HARM

WESTERN LITERATURE SERIES

T0097686

ALSO BY MILES WILSON
LINE OF FALL

HARM

POEMS

MILES WILSON

UNIVERSITY OF NEVADA PRESS, RENO & LAS VEGAS

🌱 *This project is supported by funding from the National Endowment for the Arts.*

Western Literature Series

University of Nevada Press, Reno, Nevada

89557 USA

Copyright © 1976, 1977, 1978, 1980, 1981,
1983, 1984, 1985, 1986, 1988, 1992, 1993,
1997, 2001, 2003 by Miles Wilson
Manufactured in the United States
of America

Design by Carrie House

Library of Congress Cataloging-in-
Publication Data

Wilson, Miles.

Harm : poems / Miles Wilson.

p. cm. — (Western literature series)

ISBN 0-87417-537-2 (pbk. : alk. paper)

I. Title. II. Series.

PS3573.I4598 H37 2003

811'.54—dc21   2002012292

The paper used in this book meets the
requirements of American National Standard
for Information Sciences—Permanence
of Paper for Printed Library Materials,
ANSI Z39.48-1984. Binding materials were
selected for strength and durability.

FIRST PRINTING

12 11 10 09 08 07 06 05 04 03

5 4 3 2 1

for Turner County, South Dakota
and
the McKenzie Watershed, Oregon
Where I Come From

CONTENTS

FLESH AND BLOOD

KEEPING TRACK

First we establish that life is unfair.
Any familiar story will do:
A child pedaling out from between cars.
Some bored technician, bringing the tissue sample into focus.
The man, perfectly composed now, stroking himself,
deciding
it will be the first clean-looking one,
while your wife starts home from the park
on an unaccustomed route.
The sorrow of those who tried to do most things right.

They miss the point. Which is suffering.
And randomness.

I have not forgotten the bright, tiled halls
which wait for us in official buildings,
the metallic breath of circuitry seeping
out of cool rooms, the secretary
who knows what is going to happen.

This is exact damage.
Indifferent but foretold.
Worked by the word,
syllable and subsyllable.

While God's word is His whim—
writing the book as He went. Elsewhere

some are saying "The Lord's will is my delight."
I say
be good; go to heaven.
You have a score to settle.

INTO IT

Earlier, when it was still up in the air,
in that pragmatic interval
when either of you can break it off
because no one is far enough in
to buckle on grief
like a forty-year marriage,
Darla told me her father, a city manager,
once had killed a man:
nineteen, bad luck in the wrong neighborhood.
No charges, though he caved his skull with a bat.

"Hey, killer," she'd say in bed, afterwards,
grafting my résumé onto her father
who had sized me up
like a defaulting municipal bond.
Outside, the strict iron of November
managed the city, and I played tough:
no blood tests or rubbers; no promises.

Of course, I was in over my head,
we both were,
and then she was pregnant—
bad luck in the wrong bed—
and it was a new game
playing for all the marbles
except there was another player now
and nobody could say whose team,
not even boys' or girls'
or a different league altogether.

Afterwards, she never called me "killer" again.
And when we married,
when her father handed her over at the altar,

we both knew, he and I,
who would teach a son or a daughter,
if ever there was such, to dig in at the plate.
"Good luck," he said to Darla, meaning it.
And turned back to his wife,
hopeful and baffled and thirty years into it,
in waxy light on the wooden pew.

HUSBAND IN THE GARDEN

Everything here is female
except the long, territorial stalks of corn
and they have not done well this year.
It has been cool, moist,
weather of root-swell and membrane; deep seepage,
potatoes mining their mounds.
The marriage of life and what feeds it.
This bed of earth is seasoned
with the slat and juice of my bone.

I have come out here, mindless, unnaturally calm.
"So, so, so," I say to myself
and I mean it. Let the worms have it, the weeds and weevils
make their own way. And the luminous slugs,
glistering on the damp stems.

Still, among smug and suffocating
squash, immaculate tomatoes, and posturing oriental exotics,
my intricate, tentative history brings me
barehanded
to the weave of beans.
The small mutilation leaking into the dirt
dislodges the direct
accomplishment of violence.

And row by row my homicidal eye takes me into it.
Cabbage, stupid as goats, says there is hope in loss,
you can make a beginning.
I begin with them.
Tomatoes, contrite and seeping terror,
promise me pleasure.
I, who appreciate the momentum of ruin,
go slow; snug each

fruit in my fist till the pulp seethes.
Crouched, teeth ticking,
I gouge peas from their sockets, gutter melons, nail-rake
the tissue of lettuce.
Hum a casketry: you can change your life, this garden.
Stunned onions, beets belly up, vines garroted on the wire—
all of it
quits so easily I relish the raspberries'
resistance, a little blood.

Everything is not enough
and I wade the compost pit, naked now, stained and steaming
with gore, wallowing by the armful in rot, hurling
it out to the antiseptic light and air,
the richness clotting my nostrils. A wife,
decaying, gives off resurrection.
Buried, my meat would draw maggots.
And I rise, sloughing dirt, climbing out
among the wilt and spoilage, the plunder
and green carnage, sit down on the earth,
hungry.

BAJA

Keen, bodies our knives,
whetted on tequila and the grainy sun;
honed to the edge of slaughter,
the languid sheath-time over,
we're lethal now.

Blunt beginners, clumsy at the start,
how long could we maim flesh till we struck bone?
Now we know the quick way to our thickest blood.

Here, between hawks that hunt the road
and stalled outcome of ocean,
our mutilations seep like the rabid stain of sun on sky.

You thrust your life at me.
I rise to meet you. Butcher,
I plunge myself in to the hilt.

FEWER THAN NECESSARY WORDS
CONCERNING THE END OF A MARRIAGE

So, it's done.
Eight years seems longer than it sounds.
Rage and raw love,
we vanished into fierceness at the end.
A friend once said it takes divorce
to find out how you're doing.
Now my friends are somewhere else or strange.

You write you're fine.
It's winter here.
I keep a good eye on myself,
a good eye on the hard seductive
weather coming on.
At night you loft my girls to sleep;
I lug my alien flesh from bars to beds.
Morning holds me to night's mindless bargains.

Some things still work:
nerve ends, bourbon, a few old books—
fury, guilt, despair go on
grinding,
liverish stumps of teeth in a broken mouth.
List and metaphor change nothing now.
How you unspoke my life
I can never repair with language.

How do we leave each other, then?
You, in Dallas, where your chances always were.
Me wedged in the Oregon woods,
embedded between the pit of the past,
the prowl of the future.
The geography of ending is immense.
Time leaks out everywhere.

And what did we learn?
That all we accumulated in each other could go bankrupt?
That bloodsalt stains and stings?
How what's necessary almost always happens?
No new lessons.
Just new people they're incised on.

You say you're learning how to be yourself
and liking what you learn.
Blonde sow with purple tits,
I say here's my best blessing:
go rut in another wallow.
I wish you as well as I can.

FATHERS

How did they do it,
our fathers?
Year after year
at the same job.
Coming home
to the same woman,
our mothers.
The same house.

Our fathers never
came untracked
got divorced
or fired
or thumping drunk.
Did they?

We know what it cost them.
Us.
For one thing.

And what did it get them,
weatherproofing the years?
The chance to become
four-wheel-drive Republicans?
Inexplicable sons?
Wives who side with sons
and envy their daughters' chances?
It got them that
all right.

Skidding at seventy
my father wants to know
about his life

and mine.
Careening at thirty-one
I lie
and spin the wheel
in my child's hands.

BODY

Body, old barracks; boxcar, comedian, sidekick.
Here we are, alone again,
taking what we can get.
You've brought me to the butt of my forty-third year.
You're starting to look lived in.

Old boot, bully, meatmarket.
You'd think by now we could reach some understanding.
I'm no priest, but I know this parish
like the back of my hand.
Say, for instance, those acrobatic bowels,
your perfect attendance at hangovers,
how you strut your lean metabolism.
Don't get me wrong, believe me, I appreciate
a good sneeze now and then,
being spun in delight on the shaft of sex,
this soiled blood that stiffens the eaters of grass.

Childmaker, boneyard, pissant.
For your part I know you've had to accommodate
bad posture, wives, creative abuse of organs,
poor sexual hygiene, all-night surprises,
extravagant losses of civility, dancing lessons.
You have good reason to suspect my motives,
scrawl graffiti across my moth-eaten memory,
digest your fear of my indifferent will
and standing repertoire of toxic traits.
Still, with your corny belief in our immortality
you take my picaresque defects for granted.
Plain fact, I won't always be around in a pinch.

Homeboy, hotshot, assassin.
You don't love me for myself.

You think you'd like to open up under new management.
But it's been such a long affair;
what would we do without each other?
Body, it's you and me,
the best deal we can make.

LIFE AND DEATH

The way in is always up.
I carry the gear. Ten and five, my daughters carry themselves
and don't complain much
though mosquitoes own the air
and every inch of flesh.
Into a tangle of deadfall, sidehilling it
we'll see if I still can find my way
off-trail, the topo lines on the map
old hieroglyphs: canyon, ridge, basin, pass.

> Once upon a time in country west of here
> who now cannot find his glasses
> I'd take a map, compass, and Forest Service fire pack,
> the lookout's iffy coordinates,
> find the lightning fire in the middle of everything
> and put it out.
> It seemed then ordinary enough. That's what we did
> in lives that stretched ahead forever.

With no trace of trail I am trusted absolutely
because I am their father and already they've forgotten
how I failed them. Three years ago
their mother would have been here.

> I first was trusted in these mountains twenty years ago.
> A pesky little fire, three acres maybe,
> but the main crew was gone to Idaho
> and it was night and steep and on another District.
> The men a grab bag, whoever could be rounded up.
> I'd never run a crew before.
> We cut line on it; mopped it up till morning.
> I ran around and made a lot of noise.
> Coming out when the relief driver
> lipped a tire over the gravel edge

I was awake and grabbed the wheel
and drove the rig down to the pavement and fell asleep
with my crew who couldn't know
how many years I'd sleep or worse
when I was needed.

The basin is where it's supposed to be.
I circle the pocket lake to find a campsite.
No one's been in this year—
empty tins, a broken quart of Canadian Club, the immense
    fire ring—
hunters last fall.
A resiny drift from the pines; gray jays sizing up the graft.
Sometimes I think it will be a teenager
flush from his first fuck and a six-pack
over the center line, slamming home a new cassette.
Or a spruce snag mined by beetles
on the climb out of Copper Lake,
the wind rising ahead of a squall line
the live tops dipping and springing back.

"When you die, Daddy, will you forget who I am?"

At lunch, a yellow jacket, dazed on cocoa,
too slow to fly up when I take a sip
and feel the buzzing in the coffin of my mouth
as he hammers it home.
Because I gnaw my nails, my daughter
has to pull the stinger.
It's gross and she's a little scared
but she reaches in, at the base of my tongue;
gets it on the second try.
My tongue could swell, seal off my throat,
but it doesn't.

That night I thrash up out of a dream
to the last of a dry clatter:
Claws on rock? Cougar, bear?
All the way awake I tell myself
noise is not their style,
it had to be hooves.
Still, I can't glide back to sleep
so I light the morning fire, circle the lake
to see the sun kindle Collier Glacier coming up.
Across the water the green tarp snugged above the girls—
the canopy at her gravesite—
memory's poisoned phlegm
and I have to gag it down.

Suddenly a great commotion
down at the swampy end a bear
thrashing the shallows
fishing—no, he can't hold his feet,
roiling the water
a darker color as he rips himself
on a half-sunk snag.
Some last heaves; then a hummock of fur,
black rise in the brilliant water.

We move on
over the ridge to another lake.
And it's two days of mosquitoes,
sooty eating since the pot lid vanished,
the night sky and the long silences.
Dad's amazing huckleberry biscuits.
The ordinary wonders of the world.

WHEN IT COMES

And it will,
more blunt and startling
than any metaphor of annunciation,
we take its shape:
now bluewhite neural voltage
arcing down unregulated circuitry,
now a stone
and the sludge it grinds.

We live in it frankly, our flesh
has made it manifest and our flesh
made manifest in turn.
How we are mastered
who have no place for pain
and so must be owned utterly.

Gone, and we are buoyant
as if pain's ballast had been only a heaviness
and not a rudder.
What was inscribed on the body
unreadable, not even a chart,
only an idea of chart. As if
our body might not be found
again and again.

LOCAL USAGE

THINGS TO KNOW IN WEDDERBURN

Blunt wind plunders here.
The wind and stunning rain take
whatever matters: courage, kindness, range
scoured from your life.

Here lives that have gone wrong go worse
and worse lives end in rage or toxic trance.
Bloodstreams—Rogue, Pistol, Sixes—
run thick with loss and sediment.
Six inches down you couldn't see the body.

Grief comes early here, then hardens
into stony bitterness.
Kids are tough and scrawny
dreams are scrawny
stunted things:
a bill paid up, the pickup fixed,
a twenty-dollar drunk and no hangover.
Even churches here look mean
shriveled with small sins and sour pardon.

You learn
there is a waste in wanting,
wanting more than mangled love,
more than sullen fact and taunting chances.
Women see it first
then hold the men together piecemeal.

The last thing you believe is your own life.
Absorb, survive, is what you know,
all you'll ever learn.

NIGHT BEACH SNAKE

A Sonora beach at night
barefooted
tired but only a little drunk
in the van straight through from Flagstaff.

Waves in and out, hiss and scuttle,
toy surf off the Gulf.

Then whirring
and voltage in my spine and knees
before my head.
Rattlesnake
in range.
Hair on my calves like antennae,
ears dead in the salt air,
too many chain saws, open cabs,
shrieks of crimson angels—
riff of rattles
Christ. Pay attention.
Again
but no direction.

Oh now for a cliché to live by
stropped on loss and bedroom wisdom,
what wives know:
Snakes don't strike their own.
Pray before you leap.

To stand till first light?
Hope for the tide to run in?
Beg off slantways, jump?
Our little margins
and the old questions:

How may we live our lives?
Do they sense heat or movement? Moving heat?
Could I make Nogales with the venom in?

Stepped back. Stepped again and again and
was out of it.

Back at dawn before the editorial wind.
One unbroken line of snake,
the biped's hop of faith:
one foot after the other.

And the gloss:
Pacing the night beaches
who can backtrack a career, a marriage?
Who can make Nogales with the venom in?

HARNEY COUNTY

Where muscular junipers knot against a warping wind
the willows take root, go mad, and die.
Here day and night are on the same side
and summer thunder always means it.

My grandfather's rifle rusts in the shed
because one day I heard that Winchester
withering across the tops of the sage
and the sound just kept on going.

Winter pale, the sloping coyote
hunts beyond gaunt county roads,
waits for the next lava flow,
dreams
man never came.

SHORT SEASON IN THE NORTH CASCADES

1

East from Shuksan, twelve miles
up the Siwash,
packed light, not
saying much.
Then veering from the trail
up a low-slung drainage,
climbing
until this is all that's left:
altitude, 6,000 feet,
a basin flagged with pine,
half-acre pockets of snowmelt
feeding a stream.
Light so clear, so hard,
that if I struck a rock face it
would shatter. You said once
this is how high country
sums us up.

2

We set camp
in an inlet of meadow, cropped
by a ridge's spur.
Loose from my pack I wobble buoyant
up the ridgeline—
peaks and hooded distances of fir,
a billion board feet all the way to Canada.
Below, you set up church.
Nudge the urge until
you disappear in reverence.
The choices that we make
were once our own.

3

Back down
I hack up wood, carve a firepit,
stake the tent against
a wind or snow.
You name the flowers,
scant in September
near the old snow; enshrine the south ridge,
decaying granite pilgrim,
grand mausoleum above a scalded heave of lava.
I watch that ridge,
its rock
entombed
lets go
in the daylight thaw, wheels down
reaping more stone as it comes.

4

The stream, too high, too small
for trout casts flecks of light.
I work it anyway,
get five cutthroat. We eat.
I plump our down bags in the sun.
you strip and swim
the deepest pool.
When you come from the water,
prickly with cold, I have never seen you
so naked.
I would like to.
But your blood is blank,
your flesh's face is cloistered.
It would be rape
or worse.

5

Late afternoon,
a hawk slants through the col.
Sun gluts the sky, glazes the water.
The leaves of a few stray aspen
bicker in the wind.
You tried to teach me how
to see this way.
I can, sometimes.

6

After supper I wait;
stalled between my love,
my anger.
What I am is what I need to be.
You settle up in silence. Go
to sleep as kindly as you can.
I watch, sit still, drink bourbon.
Above the ridge the night sky opens
onto final distances.

7

Morning again, gathering up, polite
as strangers. I look out
north and west
where no snow clouds have ridden up—
only a blank of sky, rock, sun,
impartial
as we let each other go.

AFTER THE BLIZZARD

Yes, I suppose the light off the snow is blue
and the hare limps, trembling etc.
A poet's supposed to register trembles and light,
a right-hander
sensing the lean of the runner at first
before he delivers.
Well here's the pitch:
Keats' rabbit has hobbled into the wrong ballpark.
You're waiting for statistics
to tell us how bad it was.
Wind chill, drift depth, records going back to 1907.
Let us not mince facts, then.
Here's one:
Soon, you will not be alive.
You can look it up.
Actuarial charts confirm folk wisdom.
Later, the whole gassy universe will sag to rest.
The second law of thermodynamics is not big news in Turner
    County
but facts
my midmost Americans
have nothing to do with who knows them.
Here's another:
What I might call this icy dome of light, this ache,
is prologue.

LIGHT AND DARK AT MEACHAM PASS

All those daybreaks. Call it fall. October.
Light come
bred to the long spread of desert and plateau.
Night, the only item on the menu,
smoke-black-going-to-blue on the mesas' flanks.
Light, the omnivore,
with a sophisticated palate for its other:
the alkaline tang of night down a Great Basin range
seasoned by sage and juniper—
sweetmeat along the water courses and rabbit haunch
creamy black in the cleft bark of cottonwood
egg sacs of dark in the bolls of piñon pine.
Leaving mannerly shadows
and never reaching underneath for all the dark
on down
beneath the great plates.

So when the light lopes on in its westerly agenda
the burred tongue of sun, a glutton rising,
strip-mines layer upon layer
bleaching the mesas immaculate
ravening dark from the gristly hides of juniper
sopping the last coagulated pools of night from the arroyos.

Engorged and drooping in its arc, this sun
cannot be everywhere and so
the debris of night,
shade of a greater dark must simply wait,
do nothing.
It is the eldest and has no shore and is the granary of itself.
First and final thing.

In the long angles of autumn, here at this divide, this
lightshed,
the line of vision sinks past the mute spectrum of winter
to the blind last sucking coming on.

WHITEHORSE RIM

Up close, a door, one-hinged,
banging hard in the wind; October
up and vagrant from Nevada.
Shingles curled or gone; crust of ice in the rutted road.
Out back, a coyote's balls nailed stiff and greasy to the shed.
Something in a heap down the ravine.
Twenty miles up-canyon
the blank and grainy eye of the falling sun,
the rancher's sister rigid from neglect.
Grit your eyes against the wind, the distance.
What happens here is final and correct.

Men who hoped and failed here named the country.
Frenchglen—Malheur River, Freezeout Mountain.
Fields—Skull Creek, Stinkingwater Pass.
Home Creek—Ten Cent Lake, Follyfarm.
Land lets us call it anything.
Our names, our wreckage, slung across it
clutter on the tongue, on paper
change maps, change nothing else.
Paiutes, teeth ground down on sand,
named it longest, said
the word for truth is weather,
is land like a patient fist.

Against this accurate sky
words flaw to whine or bellow.
Most men left, tongues gullied, humming
like wind through barbed wire.
Side with distance, weather and the seasons,
the fluency of raptors reading the air.

This country is plain speaking.
Its luck to be its own
necessity. And yours?
Say your chances
run like bad odds, your life
in the hands of some grim grammarian
obsessed with tidiness—
the land is here,
erect as the eye of a hawk.
Its imperatives your best chance
to change,
rising like the Steens from ancient faults.

BLOSSOM SHOALS, PISTOL RIVER

Traveling, traveling in the widening rain
the salmon cannot hear the salmonman.
Gulls flare west, the river rising home
rehearses night against the failing plain.
Light leaves the rain-drugged winter sky alone.

A river pocked by rain knows its own songs:
     the furling eddy, its lip of foam
     the sponging sludgy oozing of the loam
     the salmon's dirge, ecstatic monotone
The dry wash of my singing marrows bones.

Casting hard I strip the spool clean,
jam my pole in bank mud, lock the drag;
a vast Chinook will break me on a snag
and battering water up the shallowing stream
unleash me inland, release the dream
of pulpy kelp, salt-spermed root and stem.
We drift a common carcass back to them.

A GEOGRAPHY OF THE JOHN DAY RIVER

I

THE LAND

Sun erupts from the ridge like blood:
a root, a wound, a certainty.
Rock inhales the heat, patient,
swelling toward afternoon.
Summer, sledgehammer, father,
season the land is always waiting for,
sun
firing the land bonecrack dry.
The sky a greedy blue, cataract white at its rims;
wedges of cloud, shearing off the horizon,
angle for final country where I am.
Below
mangled junipers beat everything:
break stone, drain the river, outwait the sun.
The day it finally won't come up they'll be here
draped in the last tatters of the wind.
Above
ridges of rib, the land's brazed skeleton,
fractured, jammed into place, bone starkly set.
Blistered and peeled, scarped and scarred,
land that cannot be wrung from what it is;
land that will never fall from grace with itself.

A hawk cants, cuts, in the evening wind.
Light lowers like a meditation, then goes out.

II

THE RIVER

The river muscles north against the grain:
cougar-sure of what it has to do,
sinewy current flexing, unflexing,

coiled in the water
cocked in the river taut with banks.
Rock-knuckled through uplands, uncertain,
lashing its lean way to torrent
like America
plummeting
trying to get home before dark.
Immersed in how it will be above Clarno,
mindless gathering, swelling toward climax:
gouts of whitewater, gashes of canyon,
creasing recreasing
bulging through stone
hulk of wave, buckbelly curlback, careen of water,
thriving, bright seam in the fist of the land.

River, running like a crazed lover to breed with the sea:
carry my carcass, my carrion past,
less is what I need.

III

THE POET
Plundered, gutshot, gone.
Some losses cost more than you can pay.
A lusty bloodthumper, puckered in Oregon;
to say it plain, she found a better way to live.
I come out here this predatory summer,
dead-dicked, spare, not young enough.
It doesn't help much.
Country can't make anything happen
if you're really sludged up;
country got out of the lubricant business
when Wordsworth got old and regular.
Just me, John Day, Jack Daniels,
old friends who can forgive each other much.

She's back in Dallas now, married a lawyer.
I ship out for readings, watch my turpitude,
watch the lovelies sizing up my prospects
while I count breasts and meter:
two, four, six, eight,
the poet wants to fornicate.
Those shrewd, intricate locksmiths, Berryman, Roethke—
flesh is willing but the spirit fails,
quits like a bald beast driven from shelter.

If time were mercy I could tell you this:
rivers run away from me
I see my end and fear it.

BELIEVING IN TEXAS

1

Distance, first of all.
The long drift toward the Rockies, the slant
to Mexico and the Gulf.
Rising or falling the same
titanic tilt. The sky for scale.
The tall tale: lanky space, range for homespun quirks.
The corporate truth: distance owned
by signature, strands of figures
right to the edge of the map.
254 counties.

2

A man leaving his car on the Interstate, walking out,
then into wallowing trot
like a ship going down
in the trough and swell of it.
Conrad's frigate lobbing shells into Africa.

3

Presiding, a thug-like sun.
Too heavy to climb far.
The thick exhale of light
greases and burns like a film of oil
or mixes with dust to mimic the frontier.

4

Whatever must be said
rides a drawl.
A chance for words to linger
the distance that they have to go.
Or headlong Spanish
speed and spermy volume getting something through.

5

These northern words setting out with their usual mortal wounds,
fidelity or something scaling away,
desiccated by more and more—

    Houston and Hogback
    Dallas and Sinking Springs

albinos, craving pigment, remembering fall.

THE VIEW FROM FRISSEL POINT

Jim Bryant, Bob and Carolyn Moo, Mr. and Mrs. Baker.
George Paris, Mr. and Mrs. Gene Ertel, Les Rollig.
Tiny's wife, Mary.

Names cut into rock where the tower was.
Here, among debris
unburnable, too bulky to pack out,
carved deep, the lookouts in this place before me.
We only man the mountain now when thunderstorms hump in
and I am here in the thickening weather,
compass, maps, protractor, radio,
lifeguard for a hundred thousand acres
there
like a perfect model of itself.
A continuity of strangers
being here
doing this.

No more honest competition for the smokes, Jim.
Horsepasture, Castle Rock, Sand Mountain, Proxy Point
gone like log drives, ten-foot crosscut saws,
like this. Up here
tattoo of deer flies, no-see-ums and mosquitoes, drumming
of the patrol plane gridding the acres of air.
Out there, Gene,
Linton Falls still glints like mica in the sun,
the McKenzie flawed with dams and Californians.
Geometric scabs of clear-cuts
prove we're getting out the cash crop.
Fractured lightning proves hard storms
keep rolling up right on the money.

Look past
the layers of sifting light—

pumice dust can fool you on the Sisters' flanks
and ground fog wisping out of Horse Creek drainage.
But when you see real
smoke leaking up
you know it like good whiskey
like Frissel
knows the right name for itself.

Township 16, Range 8, Section 20,
the Northeast of the Southwest.
The District pivots
on my words toward the bed of fire.
I beat the patrol plane to it
and the spotter owes me a six-pack.
Mr. and Mrs. Baker, I'll buy a round.

The storm stoops east of the crest, the sky
without its ballast is enormous,
half of it over your shoulder however you turn.
Les, did you keep turning those long afternoons,
slanting away, up to the paralytic,
until your eyes
became its blank and milky blue?

Remember, Bob and Carolyn, that summer
language made you strange? Words no longer
tokens of exchange, but squinted into garble
against the distances.

George, how many people ever
undertake being alone?
The seeping into solitude,
like fasting:

first stamina, then clean embrace,
then the letting go.
What solitudes of work and marriage
changing or not changing
growing old,
hold you now out there
somewhere in America?

When you left that last season, Mary,
going down to Tiny
whose wife were you?
I'm only here odd days;
nicked by Frissel, not chiseled,
free to shout as I go down
words bannered like an oath in air:
"Pasó por aquí."

Tonight I'll be in the bar with friends
drinking one for all of you
not saying what we know:
the view from here
is durable,
more than we came to see.

ELSEWHERE

STRIPPER

North from Winnemucca, at random again,
the Dodge heaving, banging out the miles.
Peeling Santa Fe. The road goes wherever
you follow it.
I'd be in Oregon by morning.

Night corrected the empty distances, the Golconda Range
a long bone in the throat of the sky, sagebrush
belly-up against my track of sight.
Counted dead jacks until they seemed
souvenirs of a slow, bad dream.

She stopped me on an impossible straightaway,
fifteen miles at least without a dip or bend.
There, dead center, astride the line,
unbuttoned, looking half away,
persistent beyond head clearing and my rutted voice.
There.

The radio hooked Reno, stuttered and hung on.
She worked the line, the lights,
her audience.
No seamy strut or cheap moves.
Fluent, provocative as weather, a coyote
dreaming next winter's pelt, she came
out of everything.
Her last gesture was ambiguous.
Then gathering her plain clothes she stepped
beyond the cleavage of light.

Gassed up in Denio,
talked baseball with a trucker over gritty coffee.

Morning, old surgeon, entrepreneur,
got me back.
I don't know when I'll take that road again.

LAST SPRING

Here, at the surly turning of the season,
light, pale as a leper, means nothing.
Hunched in grainy corners, slush seeps like a sty.
Buds swell, uncoil; sap comes up like vomit.
Time looms in the roots, perpendicular.

Like the weather, exhausted from brawling with itself,
I'm unironic from years of stupid loss.
Clearheaded, at zero. Cycles narrow;
the year's circling closes like a throat.

At the sheer edge of spring I rehearse endings:
alone, in a room somewhere, out of money,
coughing up lung and lost chances.
On a frozen gravel road, wheels jammed,
locked in a final skid.
Ready to write the note to be found with the body
and finding there is nothing more to say.

Unsheathed, the season peels me of disguise;
my barren shadow rattles like a dirge.

IN HAND

We've come this far, a long and ugly way,
molested, carriers of husks.
Left to sort our lives with broken hands
we assemble the losses we can count
and grope the rest like Oedipus
currying his ruin in the womb,
trusting her sure feet on the open road.

We should be going down with both balls blazing,
singing, if death consumes us all what's left but life.
But when time ratchets the cogs
we lie back on the wheel and hum.

And if we should take ourselves in hand at last,
sober as any Wednesday in September,
arrange an imitation of what we should become,
then we'll learn the last prayer of the maimed,
our spiteful and insurgent flesh
still shaping, sorting out:
God take the bone.
God spare me from myself.

SANCTUARIES

these have them

Children   Asylum in delight from the world's
subpoenas

Sleek executives   At roost on their dividends

Lunar distances   Indifferent to the strut and belly
of circumstance

Hawks   Gone to breed in fathoms of air

and these

Crooked aspen   Uneconomic, secure in irrelevance

Nickel lives   Rich with tomorrow's royal flush

Abundant bastards   Finding safety in numbers

The legible blood   Biding its time, root-deep
of Indians   in the prairie sod

black with decaying sperm
six hundred river miles in
A salmon coming home
I see the bear bulk
Wavering
Above me
Gallowing
The fatal run of birthwater

RIDER

When words arced in air
Risky as cumulus
We took them into this land.

Land of lean plateau
Where all weather ends.
Enormous distances.

The hard edge of the sky
Our long neglect of need
Landscape of famishment.

The rock reveals the worm.
Light's bright pigments fade.
Night outwaits us all.

Angled into the dark
We outrage its patient pace.
Time coils to let us pass.

Sealed to a lethal ride
The rake and stain of loss
Played out along the bone

One chance whets our luck:
A hawk in the rimming sky.
We ride this cat, our breath.

NIGHTS IN CROSLEY

4 A.M.
Crosley, South Dakota.
The arthritic house
cracking its swollen knuckles,
her heart going
on, no stutter tonight.
Katie married again in Denver with her own troubles.
Karl in menswear in California.
Frederick with his father out behind the church.
The farm leased by the Jorgensens who cheat on shares.
This year only third cousins at the Fourth of July picnic.

    The land was all there was.
    We filled it with families
    then a town.
    The high school closed twelve years ago,
    the depot's gone and stores
    on Main Street quit.
    Not even kids to break the windows out.

    Wheat is empty as buffalo grass. More
    empty. Farms should mean people.

    What's left to do is finish.
    Not in the Viborg rest home, with Mrs. Rathburn,
    drooling, wearing diapers.
    Not tore down.
    Me and the town.
    This house I married in.
    What we've been
    the shaft to keep us steady,
    keep the wobble out until the end.

FOR SAN DWAYNE FRANCISCO
MISSING IN ACTION, NORTH VIETNAM

You must have looked as big as America, looming
beneath your chute above their fields,
enlarging in the fertile air
coming down, the land blooming with craters, colors
as though your whole life had been
black and white.

I heard years later from a high school friend:
your wingman saw the chute seed;
he had ground contact.
Then the decay of silence.

In the end the names:
American, pilot, criminal.
Drought, flood, plague.
Names that twisted their lives,
blackened their tongues.
How could they believe your own—
blind dates, bartenders, colonels never did—
detect in bland, professional hands
seasons of nail and knuckle,
a farmer's knowing how
grace and grief come
from the sky?

How could they know you
unintentional as frost? A pilot by accident
of reflex, harrowing with rocket pods and cannon,
the only tools in all those acres of air.

May crops grow where you are
in that extravagant country, lavish
as Benton County wheat is plain,
your right life
leaching shrapnel from the earth.

JOE, DEAD

In Memoriam, Joseph Schoenfeld, 1948–1980

It could have happened this way or another.
Done, it makes no difference. Still
crossing, a block from home,
after another six-pack. Jesus, Joe,
you knew better. Knew it
another small loss to bulk.
We didn't need the lesson
in how our appetites consume us,
inviting whatever wishes us ill in this world.

This time no time
to scout the water
say "No deal, no deal";
pull against the current angling
for a crafty way through.
Too slow to pivot, the bigger you are
the less chance.
Nothing to fall back on then except your luck
which was never good.

Of course, there's the mess.
Now or eighty.
Friends, family, lovers left in disarray.
Nothing settled, details piling up. A shambles.
Our histories rocking in your wake.
Does a rising river pucker between banks?
Spring weather pick up after itself?
You spilled over everywhere.

At the memorial the McKenzie looked like itself.
Your mother read those sappy poems,
your brother so much like you it could have been

a bad joke.
Everyone wondering
who was the tattooed woman, the man in the suit.
Everyone saying
"Remember how wonderful Joe was?"
Well, that is true
and other things besides. Still
beyond all quarrel
your vivid girth,
a substantial fact of nature
to be reckoned with.

Some losses must be accounted for.
Idiot Death, slobbering, snot-smeared,
out for a good time Saturday night
puking from envy
did this.
After the first death there is no forgiving.

HOW IT HAPPENS

Down from the flint plateau
Bearing greased skulls of their mothers
Bearing themselves as a tribe
When they come to the estrus of plunder

At the loins of the World-Provider
The birthwater of our Great River
They squat chewing dung in a trance
Carving the hemlock graveships

That will carry the flesh of our singer
When he casts his flute to the fire
When he pierces his drum with a brand
And goes to them full of the singing

All we have ever remembered.
When the graveships come we are nothing
Trackless as mist on the water.
They do what they must in contempt.

The one we wound they abandon
His rage curves over the world
Curves his bright hand to the knife
That must trick our past from the willow
Curves his keen tongue to the song
The oldest man had forgotten.

VITA

We really shouldn't
hold Death's job against him.
He gets bored,
like us,
doing the same thing
year after year.
Doesn't like to get up in the morning
for appointments in Samarra
or Dubuque.
Knows he should get more
exercise and eat less.
Doesn't see much prospect
for advancement.

Sure,
he's not much fun at parties
but imagine
what it would do to your personality
to be considered
inevitable,
allowed to repeat yourself
indefinitely,
never be invited
to join the Chamber of Commerce.
I believe,
all things considered,
Death hangs in there pretty well—
not always flashy
but a real credit to his profession.

That's pretty much it,
unless

you missed the free samples
and last night's interview:
Death is not looking forward
to retirement.

BEAR ON THE STUMP

Considering the threadbare show of the U.S. Forest Circus,
the general lack of victuals and vision,
in fact, the whole unsavory state of the Union,
the bear resolves to eat his congressperson
or in the same civic spirit
run for office.
The Big One.

The bear

> Grooms himself in a wallow, imagining a Democratic
> fund-raiser.
> Dines on salmon; fancies himself a Republican.

> Scruffs around under a log for termites and a media man.

> Agrees to "The Bear Went Over the Mountain" as his campaign
> song
> sung *al dente* to the tune of
> "I Did It My Way" or "Bolero."

> Bids adieu to the chronic boredom of living among bosky
> ungulates.

> Squeezes his privates until he yelps with sincerity
> the right tone for network coverage.

> Ponders his campaign slogan:
> "A Bear of the People"
> "Why Not the Bearest?"
> "Bearifest Destiny"
> "The Only Candidate Who's Part of Our National Heritage"

Settles on
   "Bear with Me"

Breaks joyous wind upslope from the Baptist camp,
a position paper on the separation of Church and State.

Practices the right inflection for "My fellow critters."

Broods about his image:
The slander concerning his ties with Wall Street.
That garbage-dump incident at McKenzie Bridge.
And the Goldilocks business—
though he now has a testimonial from the divine Ms. G.—
   that little twit—
which should help him out with the fairy-tale lobby.

Announces Herbert Xavier J. Edgar Cougar as his running
   mate.
Though he has been advised to balance the ticket
with an invertebrate
the nation is not yet ready
for a literally spineless VP.

Relishes the headlines:
   "Bear Scores Pols"
   "Bear Touts Teeth for EPA"
   "*Ursus* versus Taxes: Bear Urges Budget Slash"
   "Bear Promises Spring"
   "Bear Baits Opponent"
   "Omnivores Give Bear Nod"

Would proclaim himself king, promise a participatory monarchy,
but huckleberry diarrhea keeps him humble.

Posed in his den with the works of A. A. Milne
and the *Reader's Digest* condensed Constitution
prominently displayed,
grants an interview:
"My wit? The only thing more pungent is weasel piss."
Denies the quote.

Trips the light fantastic,
800 pounds of glee and gluttony, imagining graft.

Gropes a Sierra Club groupie at a campaign bash.

Squints at the horizon, statesmanlike,
planning a bipartisan menu for State dinners.

YOU, THEODORE ROETHKE

Baboon and buzzard; lizard, lamb, and shrew
Abound when I root round my furnished zoo.
I celebrate the small. When I'm outdoors
I turn to grass before the carnivores.

I keep my Yeats at home beside John Clare
And take my metaphysic from the air.
In lean times I light out for the far fields,
Wolf down what princely toad or toadstool yields.

I knew a woman once but then forgot
Myself. Our aerobatic turkey trot
Ground to a waltz that I had danced before.
I recollect myself upon the floor.

I listen for my bones' prophetic rattle,
Stay out of swimming pools around Seattle.
Contortionist, I'm hanging tough and loose,
A slick, corkscrewing gander to time's goose.

My journeys bear me through the neighborhoods
Of outermost and intimate, dark woods.
I've molted till there's nothing left to shed
And learned by going where to go instead.

HEFTING IT

GETTING THERE

Start with this:

   A bag of earth.
You can
grow food, cover
your tracks, pitch it up
to get the drift
of the wind.

   A source of light.
For you will be doing much
night traveling.
Money is luminous
and may be otherwise useful.

A good hat is handy—
sheds sun and water.
Wool is best.
You may pass for an animal
or pull it over your eyes.

Attitude is important.

Take for your text
the strut and belly of circumstance.
Remember everything
pretends to obey the laws of gravity.
Learn the gait
of give and give and give and give
and get.

Keep a change of scruples.
If you run low

make-do
is the first law of the road.

Travel light, but not alone;
tracked by the scavengers of stumble
a companion may prove club-footed.
The road lives on
the sure thing.

You may wish to develop
a sense of direction
to avoid circling home:
Moss grows on the north side of the dead.
Inquisitory light rises in the east.

Trust distance.

Some say
stick to thickets,
the legs go first.
Others advise high ground,
claim the heart. They may be right.

Learn to distinguish
between salt water and fresh.
Both may kill you
but one will.

Carry some luck to fall back on
in case
you ever make a mistake.

Don't tell anyone how you came.

THE WILL TO FAIL

It appears without notice
like sleeping without falling from bed,
something you can take no credit for.

Say your life has lurched along ramshackle
like one of those Mexican buses
running by the rickety grace of God
from blunder to breakdown.

Your first suspicion is a small unfocusing:
a spike of urgent sound in the empty house
a taint in the rising wind of sour city rain
a dream in which you cannot remember something important.

It will become a sure presence:
the stale gray of your morning breath
grease behind the stove
a splinter edging in.

Later, when you are introduced at a party,
the name is familiar; the face reminds you of someone.

Soon it is perfectly domestic, shambling
around the house like an old dog; familiar
as the bathroom light switch, unobtrusive
as a book you haven't read in years, habitual
as your side of the bed.

Its talents are at your disposal.
Agile, it unlimbers metaphors:

It is frugal as a cat walking away
spending no more effort than it must.

It is shrewd, like a good gambler,
letting you win enough to stay in the game.

It knows more proverbs than your high school coach:
When the going gets tough, the tough get going.
Loss builds character.
Bad luck is better than no luck at all.

Though by nature promiscuous
it is a faithful lover in its fashion
who will be with you
always.

TAKING STOCK

Insolvent, my unaudited self-worth
seeks credit in the affluence of friends.
One exhorts: retrench, divest, unload
your low-yield scruples and a guilt or two.
Like unencumbered blondes, a lean portfolio is lots more fun.

A second counsels go for broke,
procure a hand that feeds you, bite it.
Sell yourself short. Refuse all offers.
Improvidence can open up all sorts of new perspectives.

An old abundant lover writes that I was always in arrears.
Another says you've buttered your own bread,
now lie in it.
Long after debts are canceled I still turn my pockets out.

My landlord touts a seminar that recommends sound management—
hale balance, hearty ego.
I could resolve to change my delinquent habits,
straighten up and out.
Frugal, I could walk to bars instead of driving.

Bankrolled in bourbon, I consult my oracular bottle.
The bottle says you're not the fraud
that one good woman couldn't fix.
The barmaid says pay up.

I swear some days the swindling past was possible:
old bankbooks, fellowships, my time in the half-mile;
even the blue-chip woman
who left for her good reasons
once liked me well enough to marry.
Memory's deposit is my only asset now.

Alone, at home, I sleep a lot.
In my luxurious dreams
the bandit banks of time do not foreclose.
Awake, I promise I'll be richer soon.

Bold from repetition all my blunders jeer and cackle.
The windfall losses gather at my throat.

DRUNK

He never hit her
though he patiently knocked her back
out of his life.
Which wife?
Well, actually, both, if you count the last one.
Everybody else did.

He never busted a window or kicked in a door
though he burned the house down.
Lost your books and mss. in that one.
A lesson learned: stash copies somewhere else.
Too bad you couldn't stash a copy of yourself, eh?

He never got nailed driving drunk.
Out of how many times?
Three hundred, nine hundred. Who keeps track?
How much is left in the bottle in the garage?

He was only sort of fired once for drinking
or once fired sort of for drinking.
Back on your feet in what—three years? Of course, you were younger then.

He never got the shakes.
There's one for the obituary.

His children never saw him drunk.
We don't really want to get into the children, do we?

Never vodka or NyQuil or Sears' best bourbon-flavored paint
    stripper, Old Mortuary.
The Sodality of Elegant Western imbibers.

He tried, God knows, thirty intricate years: two beers a day,
no hard stuff, once a week, not before dawn, eight years stone
cold, Prozac, therapy, a higher spiritual power, astrology,
factories of sugar, the liver's annual bad news, threats, promises,
bribery, bargains, lists—Jesus, the lists—amulets of chums and
family gone soddenly down, always with aspirin and milk thistle
and B-complex, only in celebration, only in misery, only in
boredom, never, never, never
Keep talking, pal.

THESE DAYS

These days I have little,
waking up without
even a hangover
to instruct my conduct,
having called it quits
the world returns
the favor. There is, of course, a modest inventory
of neglect: eyes gone cocked, teeth rusted through,
poor spiritual hygiene and the quag
of memory, like gray meat
going bad on the bottom shelf.
Everywhere I went I learned something.

The things nobody talks about
in poems, for good reason, I suppose: Christmas.
Swaggering 19th-century sunsets.
Getting a job—the fist-stuffed-
in-the-leaking-life variety.
Or not getting a job.
Sitting around. Sleeping later and later.

The piggish childheartedness of doing
something utterly useless like
waiting for grace or mercy,
like this.

How does the world so often
inept in other matters
smell you out unerringly
and cruise on past?
People who did it right waving—
yes, some waving
and fondling their tangibles
at the same time.

To behave steadfastly
in such circumstance
is a violation of natural law.
Whatever is possible
must be
accomplished.
Everywhere
I go
I learn the same thing.

SLASH BURNING

It goes like this—
forty acres, give or take,
of bedlam. A derangement of land
called clear-cut.
True naming at eye level, but lower
in the region of sperm and egg
and on down a bewilderment:
gaping stumps, the rot and shatter
of trunks, pitch leaking, congealed,
every digit
and the needle hair of each pore.
The dirt astonished.

I walk this mountainside
groin-deep in carnage,
drooling splatters of fire.
What will happen here?
Something surgical, not precise but
cauterant, perhaps
a benediction.

Seamless
fire spreads its litany
along the barkskin, finding each crevice:
Mine, it chants, *Mine* and *Now.*
Walloping up the slope
ignites its undersong:
More.
Everything.
Logs and rocks tearing free.
Evidence
going up in smoke.

I am the element.
This hillside's only season.
Man of fire,
sweating as I correct the natural world.

EVIDENCE

Crows veer off, roots warp away, aspen leaves hold still.
Deep in the pocket of sleep, a woman shivers.
Small Dakota towns say I never lived there.
Even the spiny seduction of pain furls its thistle.

What you could not praise forsakes you.

My prints in the crisp sand ooze like wounds.
Air hemorrhages around my festering breath.
Long grass withers in the slit of my shadow.
My replica slurs water; at my gesture fire forgets its names.

You damage what you do not understand.

Light thins around me as I move.
At night, cased in a mute, leprous glow,
I lurch from the fleshy breast of dark.

Unspeakable. The right word rotting on your tongue.

MOSTLY NOT

Those days I got up mostly
drunk in the dark
and drove the McKenzie
pouring coffee from the Stanley between the curves
steering with my thighs
and logged
or way down on my luck
worked the Forest Service.
A wiry, savage wreck of a man
who looped a choker around his waist,
climbed hung-up firs—
sometimes I closed my eyes,
rose by feel and fear alone—
snagged the piece of bad luck so the skidder could pull it free.
Come down so gone I couldn't tell
I'd crapped up there
unless I groped my jeans.

These days
I come in at ten
to where a committee meeting, however it smells,
beats a poke in the eye with a sharp stick.
And you never look
where first light falls
up Wapiti or Frissel to see
if you'd be logging today in rain or snow.

Who I worked with then I called friend
or asshole
and answered for it.
Now I have colleagues
who scurry and flush
when the shit comes down

which it does, always descented,
from assholes way beyond my repertoire.
My colleagues mostly mean well—
they have families after all—
so you can't just beat the shit out of them
or, in the unlikely instance, vice-versa.
You wonder if they used to amount to anything.
At night just me and the janitors.
All of us Vietnam but me
the only one with a V.A. mortgage.

My colleague at Santini Brothers,
former Lance Corporal Whatcott,
wore this tattoo beneath his *Semper Fi:*
>   *When I die bury me face down*
>   *so everybody can kiss my ass*
I hope they did.

Sometimes at night I go out in my backyard
with a bottle and swear out loud.
But mostly not.

THE FALL

Narrative mostly in place—my fifties a seasoning
of my forties into the years to come—
thicker, less nimble, a little drifty but durable
    out in it

Separation Creek
some last low-elevation old growth
Three Sisters Wilderness.
The Cyclopic canopy, stand and deadfall behind,
the riotous creek before.
Brush and fastfall
as always
no room to cast
as always
years of minimal technique.
Dimples of light
muting the leader and #10 flies just out
of bifocal range.
The water an old text
I can read by heart.

   The world suddenly otherwise—
knowing better the instant before I go through
a crotch of duff sloughed off two criss-crossed firs eight feet
    over rock.
Ribs, shoulder, ankle
goners for sure.
Filaments of pain and shards of dark when I move.
The cold pragmatic:
too far in to crawl out.

Then, by gingerly fraction, everything
seems to work.

Though later deep harm in the liver
and finally no more booze.

The lessons yet to come,
the story's end
will be told by the body.

OUT OF

—for Philip Levine

Out of hoarfrost and mercy.
Out of the long luck of marriage—
the gesture behind the children at breakfast
and the return of gesture.
Out of mistakenness.
Out of Boxcar Summit, the West opening like a fairy tale,
the East a sermon receding,
a debt somebody else owes.
Out of tedium and grace and beholdenness.
Out of the brown curds of blood swirling in the bowl.
Out of work so wrong only you can be found to do it right.
Out of kiss-my-ass.
Out of stain and forgiveness.
Out of thanksgiving for appetite which does not
resemble wreckage. Out of wreckage
which does not resemble a diary.
Out of Mobile and Scranton, Muncie and Spokane.
Out of the steadfastness of place and the mutagens of desire.
Out of God's compact: sizzle of rain in the burning socket.
Come.

THE RISING

Stunned, in a sullen parch,
The banded heart denies
All liquid but its own.

Pumps from its salt pulp
Corrosive, nourishing brine
While veins forget the sky.

Veins that swell with surprise
When the weather of a woman
Lengthens into a season—

Love rises around my knees
My groin is wet with forgiveness
I can learn to breathe under water

KATE, IF YOU COME

Rain that rakes these months
Releases me from need
Of what I'll never be.

Here, in the grief of weather,
The thin eye of winter,
I peel to my last roots.

Change blunders through our lives,
Blood goes stiff with loss
And certainty of endings.

We render what remains,
This calendar of flesh
Where everything comes true.

For flesh is what we have
Against time's vacant lust,
Flesh and the leap of language—

I inhabit myself like fire.
Bank me in your body.
Luck rises from my ashes.

BODY SONG

The will of my cells is my will.
Shall I swear this will is my own?
Earth's clockwork is hounding me, still
I abound and elude its grave tone.

My sperm is as quick as a thief.
I'd burn to enlighten the sun.
I delight in the whet of my teeth
And devour my luck as it comes.

I believe in the arc of my bones—
The timbre along my tuned skin—
They hammer this flesh for its songs.
Dark peals where my body begins.

My blood is electric with chance;
Incandescent, a spectrum of change.
The weave of my veins winds a dance
And I dance it till nothing is strange.

WHY GOD MUST PERMIT EVERYTHING

God's preference, of course, inclines to the righteous.
But truth be told—more as Yahweh the Yid, the Hebrew Hammer,
than as the Good Old Goy, that New Testament Featherweight—
the Pugilist of Paradise fancies a rip-roaring spiritual scrap.

Which requires, of course, the truly bad.
Provisioned with wherewithal etc. etc.
So Satan, so voice mail, so automatic transmissions
and Zero Coupon, Connecticut. So the old Nixon,
the new Windows, the perpetual New York Mets:
plenty of roughage for the moral digestion.
Necessary and familiar to the Grand Projectionist
as Jesus' dog (that faithful hound of heaven
scrubbed out of the Gospels in the fourth century
by the Nicene Council, replaced with lambs, asses, fish, whatever).
So agony, unspeakable practices, mortal and immortal sin
explicable to the most dense and Christ-ridden congregation.

But the middling? Considered only by fringe spiritual cranks.
How does the Lord of Extremity,
the Master of Magnitude, permit the quotidian?
The sharp and the blunt
but also the dull,
the tepid, the middle register, Nebraska?

Left to its own devices, the midmost
suffocates the extremes
like a sow rolling languidly on its brood.
For instance, the minute God's attention is diverted—
say He's parting the Red Sea or rigging
the Saturday night Knights of Columbus bingo game—
a saint shimmies down from his pillar of salt,
some middle-management fallen angel

sculls off from the Burning Lake,
and before God can say "Jehoshaphat"
they've moved to Catatonia, Indiana
where they marry, maintain the third-best average
in the Thursday-night mixed-doubles league.

Therefore that hot-or-cold-okay-but-lukewarm-
I-spit-out-of-My-mouth business:
a crabby misunderstanding
before the Kid got the big picture.

His laws of thermodynamics now command
that everything tends to the temperate.
What did you think
that shapeless, relentless, neither/nor mass comprising
most of the Christian universe
is
if not the mediocre?
In fact, an intriguing passage in the Book of Ralph
from the Apocrypha fingers the ordinary—
that raw though not libidinous material—
to be the very stuff
out of which God fashions the uttermost.

So God must permit this poem.

HORSEPASTURE MOUNTAIN LOOKOUT
WAPITI RIDGE

Men give names
then take
what they name away.
The pasture gone to trees,
trees to clear-cuts.
Horses in parades.
Below Lamb Butte
Weyerhaeuser saws
find what coyotes never touched—
the stiff lip of firs on English Mountain
strikes the flag.
The lookout, a snarl of cable,
shroud of glass, wood sludge and slag of iron.
The mountain
girdled now by pavement
remembers Wapiti meant elk.
To translate asphalt
you must know some malicious foreign tongue.

A forester disfiguring trees into board feet
says "Next year we'll have this new machine."
But the last bear who passed through said
"Be kind, sleep when you can.
The sky here still
is wide as the mouth of God.
The wind comes likes a blind, enormous drunk
and you may have noticed boxcar rocks
on Forest Service Road one-six-six-seven."

"My sources indicate that the South Fork's
sucking at the dam
and glaciers grow by tons above
the sovereign Sisters' yeast of lava."

"I plan to breed next season."

PROVISIONS

Now I turn back.
The past, which I had laid down,
I lift up again in my hands
not like a blade at the wrist
not a gradient of regret, thread of spittle and ash,
but an old rib, bread and fire on the tongue.

I

THE GROUND AT HURLEY
My grandmother, her husband, father, sisters;
her mother, her infant son
in the ground at Hurley.
South Dakota farmland in every direction,
some of it mine. Alien
in these fields going on
without the clever grandson
who sang at two,
Christmas Eve in the Presbyterian Church,
joy to a world
which has harvested
every Woodward, every Rundell.
The family house
sold, then rented, then boarded up.

The clever grandson
banging together the living and the dead
furiously
to no applause
from men who bribe the irrigated corn
with tons of chemicals and fossil water.
All walloping the machine
until *tilt* flashes up
and every light goes out.

Elsewhere, wind tears back the scab of the sky
which we cannot bandage
with *yes, yes,*
but a sturdy midcontinent *maybe,*
harrowing under *whatever,*
stitching up the mouths of *God, please, no.*
A *maybe* fed on potatoes and corn
and a roast on Sunday—
Presbyterian Sundays and the visible odds:
Everybody here has made it this far.

II

M C K E N Z I E   B R I D G E
Hunkered down on Frissel Point
hair lifting up,
the ozone, God's breath, on me.
Then the worst of it past
the smokes coming up and I call them in
naming this combustible creation:
township, range, section.

All over the West, Jesus, imagine it.
I've got slides and stories.
Everything around you fire, fuel, or wick:
weariness a wick, bad luck, courage
wicking you to the bluewhite point
where it's all rapid oxidation
and metaphysics.
Paso Doble and Nat Spencer cutting line
till the saw bar warped with the heat.
Crider Creek where we held a south-slope run
in ponderosa slash with half a crew.
Cleaning the Missoula jumpers out of the bar

on R & R at Schoolhouse. Rincon and
Captain Prairie; Rebel Rock and Cain.
It makes this body ache and ring.
And I store it up,
jerky and lime; sweetmeat,
root, berry, and stem
provisioning this ark of bones
as it bears its cargo away
to the master of waters.

Packing out from Proxy Ridge
a loping downhill stride.
Okay, some blisters and pretty tired, okay
the new kid talks too much
but the fire's out.
A brimming rises up through the valley haze . . .
down there my bed and Gretchen
tomatoes ripe in a week
my beat-up fly rod, three days off—
music I fit into like old jeans.
The lyrics:
Like this, yes, as you are.
And here.

STARTING FROM HERE

Surely, I am neither too old nor able
for setting out
in this America
where last week's versions, all the tarnish of as-is,
are unballasted as we sail buoyantly off
with their glittering inversions,
the next booth at the carnival.

Let's say you start from where you are
if you can find it:
dim, stagnant ground beneath a pungent moral thicket.
This one unkempt except for his iambic jaw.
A history of threadbare postures, clumsy misdemeanor, a life
that will not heal.

I'll start by not rehearsing fifty
perhaps with some dactylic strut,
rip-roaring lines that sizzle at the edges.
Or the level tongue of the rain.
By rattle and crow, bluff and weasel
I'll make things up, fondle figures of speech,
wear the enigma down with windiness,
whatever it takes—
Consistency becomes homogenous hum, a recitation.
You get the same surprises every time.
Why, the air itself is uneven.

And this assortment—
        squall and operatic hoot
        the standard griefs
        truth croaking like a buzzard, a passenger pigeon,
        ill-tempered, avoidably clever
        smudgy ego all over everything

the political engagement of a sweat sock
and up to its green gizzard in woodsiness.
Still, some chancy saying-so
breathtaking stunts
love and a few laughs—
come word by word to be
the work of a grown man.

THE PROMISE KEEPERS

We come like memory,
that shaft on which we turn, wheeled by the past
geared coils of motive, guilt, and blame.
We come, obedient as water
to those we love and no longer love,
those who can call us to living account
and the dead.
Across the watershed of moral age
we belong less to ourselves
than to an intricate field of promises;
like gravity, like natural law
we slope to them.

Promises that support us, even against ourselves, light
doubled by the river.
Promises that use us up, like a long illness,
with no expectation of mercy.
Promises we inherit like a genetic oath.
Promises that enfold us, cradling against the urgency
of chance and change or fix us, still twisting, to the felt,
the glass already sliding into place.
While time, our devout custodian, bears us up and along,
the itch of circumstance cruising in murky jags.

And the world whispers *sucker*
and parades the merits of adjustment, the plausible harvest
of opportunity, singing the provisional
anthem of itself.
What can we know?
Only what the world exacts
and our countersong,
the keeping.

ACKNOWLEDGMENTS

Grateful acknowledgment is made to the editors of the following journals in which versions of these poems first appeared:

Bellingham Review: "Whitehorse Rim"
Cimarron Review: "Last Spring"
The Georgia Review: "Why God Must Permit Everything"; "The Promise   Keepers"
Interdisciplinary Studies in Literature and Environment: "Life and Death"; "McKenzie Bridge"; "The View from Frissel Point"
Kansas Quarterly: "Bear on the Stump"
Manhattan Poetry Review: "Evidence"
The Massachusetts Review: "Mostly Not"
New Mexico Humanities Review: "For San Dwayne Francisco: Missing in Action, North Vietnam"
New Orleans Review: "You, Theodore Roethke"
The New York Quarterly: "Baja"
The North American Review: "Into It"
North Dakota Quarterly: "Nights in Crosley"
Oregon Times: "Things to Know in Wedderburn"
Poetry: "Body"; "Stripper"
Poetry Northwest: "Night Beach Snake"; "Slash Burning"
The Sewanee Review: "Getting There"; "Husband in the Garden"
Southern Poetry Review: "The Will to Fail"; "Kate, If You Come"
The Texas Observer: "These Days"; "Believing in Texas"
Western Humanities Review: "Harney County"
Writers Forum: "Fathers"; "In Hand"; "Vita"